I PLEDGE ALLEGIANCE

by June Swanson

pictures by
Rick Hanson

Carolrhoda Books · Minneapolis

To my husband, Stan
With love and gratitude

This book is available in two editions:
Library binding by Carolrhoda Books, Inc.
  a division of Lerner Publishing Group
Soft cover by First Avenue Editions,
  an imprint of Lerner Publishing Group
241 First Avenue North
Minneapolis, MN 55401 U.S.A.

Website address: www.lernerbooks.com

Library of Congress Cataloging-in-Publication Data

Swanson, June.
    I pledge allegiance / by June Swanson ; pictures by Rick Hanson.
  Rev. ed.
        cm. — (On my own history)
    Summary: Describes how and why the Pledge of Allegiance was
  written, how it has changed in wording over the years, and precisely
  what it means.
    ISBN: 0–87614–925–5 (lib. bdg. : alk. paper)
    ISBN: 0–87614–912–3 (pbk. : alk. paper)
    1. Bellamy, Francis. Pledge of Allegiance to the flag—Juvenile
  literature. 2. Flags—United States—Juvenile literature. [1. Pledge of
  Allegiance.] I. Hanson, Rick, ill. II. Title. III. Series.
  JK1759.B383S93 2002
  323.6'5'0973—dc21   2001007313

Manufactured in the United States of America
  3 4 5 6 7 – JR – 08 07 06 05 04

The 1880s were exciting years
for the United States.
Henry Ford was building a buggy
that would run on gasoline.
Electric lights were being put
into stores, offices, and homes.

In Chicago, one of the first
skyscrapers was built.
It was an amazing 11 stories high.

Some frontier areas
were soon to become states—
Montana, Washington, North Dakota,
South Dakota, Idaho, and Wyoming.
In a short while, the country
would have 44 states in all.

During these years, there was
a magazine for children
called *The Youth's Companion*.
It came once a week to homes
across the United States, and
it was filled with adventure stories.
One week in 1888,
the children opened their magazines
and found a special project.
The Youth's Companion
was asking them to help buy
United States flags for their schools.
The children must have liked the idea.
They collected enough pennies
to buy 30,000 flags.

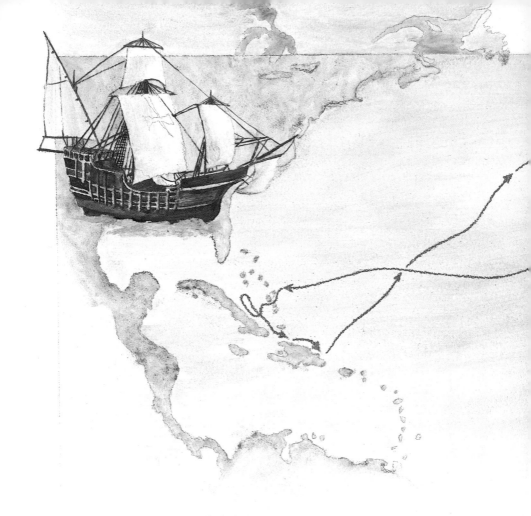

The Youth's Companion
had more ideas for the children.
The year 1892 was coming soon,
and in that year, America
would have an important anniversary.

Exactly 400 years earlier,
Christopher Columbus had sailed
across the Atlantic Ocean from Spain.
On October 12, 1492, he landed at
a place many people had never heard of.

This land came to be called America.
The Youth's Companion
wanted to celebrate the 400th
anniversary of Columbus's arrival.
So two men from the magazine,
Francis Bellamy and James Upham,
began to plan a school celebration.
It would be called Columbus Day.
Children across the United States
would raise their new American flags
over their schools.
Together they would say
something to honor the flag.

Columbus Day grew closer.
Francis Bellamy traveled
to Washington, D. C., to talk
to President Benjamin Harrison
about the celebration.
The president liked the idea.
He made Columbus Day
a holiday for the whole country.

Francis Bellamy still had
one more thing to do.
On a warm evening in August 1892,
Bellamy sat down to write
something to honor the flag.
When he finished,
his salute was only one sentence long:

I pledge allegiance to my Flag
and to the Republic
for which it stands—
one Nation indivisible—
with liberty and justice for all.

A few weeks later, the children read
the salute in their magazines.
It was called
The Youth's Companion Flag Pledge.
There were only 23 words,
but some were long and hard.

Teachers helped their students
understand the words.
First, the children learned that
a **pledge** is a promise.
They were promising **allegiance**.
But what did allegiance mean?
The teachers explained that allegiance
means to love and be true to something.

And what was that something?

It was the flag and their country.

The teachers explained that the flag

is a symbol, or a sign,

that stands for the United States.

So in the pledge, the children

were promising to be true

to the United States and

to help it any way they could.

Republic was another hard word.

It is the kind of government

the United States has.

In a republic, everyone can vote

for the leaders in the government.

Nation was pretty easy.

It is another word for country.

19

Then came **indivisible**.

Indivisible means that something
cannot be divided or pulled apart.
Thirty years earlier, the United States
had been in a terrible civil war.

It was a war between the northern
and the southern states.
But even this war had not been able
to pull apart the United States.
The nation was indivisible.

Most of the children knew the word
liberty, which means freedom.
Before the Civil War,
some people in the United States
had been slaves.
But slavery was no longer allowed.
Everyone now had liberty.
Justice was the last word to learn.
It means being fair and
having the same laws for everyone.
The children now understood that
they were promising to help
the government of the United States
give freedom to all and
treat people fairly.

When Columbus Day finally came,
the children were ready.
Twelve million schoolchildren
across the country recited the salute.
As Francis Bellamy listened,
6,000 children in Boston
roared it out together.
It made him happy and
proud of his country.
In a short time,
children were saying it
every morning at school.
It became known as
The Pledge of Allegiance.

By 1912, the pledge was 20 years old,
and the country was still growing.
Henry Ford's "gasoline buggies"
were now called automobiles.
Each month his factories
made 26,000 of them.

Orville and Wilbur Wright
were working on their first airplane.
The expedition of Robert Peary
had planted an American flag
near the North Pole.
Four more states in the West
had joined the nation.

They were Utah, Oklahoma,
New Mexico, and Arizona.
This made a total of 48 states.
The country had changed much
over the past 20 years,
but the pledge had stayed the same.
Now the pledge
was in for some changes too.

In 1923, a group of men
who had fought in American wars
called a meeting to make rules
about ways to honor the flag.
The people at this meeting looked carefully
at *The Pledge of Allegiance.*
They felt the words of the first line
could be confusing.
When someone said,
I pledge allegiance to my flag,
what flag did the person mean?
So the people at the meeting
changed the first line to:

*I pledge allegiance to the flag
of the United States of America.*

They also decided that
everyone should say the pledge
with their right hands on their hearts.

As the pledge became more important,
people began to argue about
who had written it.
Francis Bellamy said he had.
Others said James Upham had.
But in 1939, the argument ended.
The United States Flag Association
declared Francis Bellamy
the official author of
The Pledge of Allegiance.

Three years later, in 1942,
the United States was
fighting in World War II.
Automobile companies had
stopped making cars.
Their factories now made
trucks, tanks, and war planes.

Women and retired men went to work
in factories and shipyards.
Steel pennies and silver nickels
were used for money.
In October of 1942,
the pledge became 50 years old.
During this special birthday year,
Congress made the pledge official.
The Pledge of Allegiance—the little
salute written for the children of 1892—
was now part of national law.
After this, only the government
could change the pledge.

Though *The Pledge of Allegiance* was official, it was still causing arguments. Several states had laws saying that children must begin each school day by reciting the pledge.

Some people did not like this.
They believed allegiance
should be pledged only to God.

In 1943, the most important court in
the United States, the Supreme Court,
made a decision.
No one—child or adult—
could be forced to say
The Pledge of Allegiance.
To *make* someone say it was against
liberty and justice for all.

In 1954, Congress was once again
arguing about the pledge.
One congressman, Louis Rabaut,
wanted to add the words
"under God" to it. He pointed out that
President Abraham Lincoln had called
the United States "this nation, under God"
in *The Gettysburg Address*,
a famous Civil War speech.

We here highly resolve that
these dead shall not have died
in vain—that this nation under
God, shall have a new birth of
freedom—and the government of
the people, by the people, for the
people shall not perish from

Representative Rabaut thought the words
from *The Gettysburg Address*
would sound good in the pledge.
Some people didn't agree.
They felt a belief in God should be kept
separate from the laws of the country.
So Congress took a vote on it.
They decided to have the pledge say
one nation under God.
This was the pledge's last change.

Americans look to their flag as
a symbol of their country.
It stands for unity and strength.
In times of trouble, the American flag
and the Pledge of Allegiance have
special importance.

Many things have changed since
the pledge began in 1892.
But the love Americans have for
their country has not changed.
And Americans of all ages still promise
to support their country when they say:

I pledge allegiance to the flag
of the United States of America
and to the Republic
for which it stands,
one Nation under God,
indivisible,
with liberty and justice for all.